Athletes' Devotional

You Can Do All Things...

366 Days of Biblical Inspiration for Athletes of All Pursuits
Plus 100 Bonus Encouragement Scripture Passages
Includes Subject Index

Compiled by
Brian Stauffer

Dedication

Dedicated to my wife, Shelley; our parents who went before us; our children; and our grandchildren. And most importantly, this devotional is dedicated to our Lord and Savior, Jesus Christ.

Acknowledgements

The NIV (New International Version) of the Bible in Bible Gateway was used with occasional verses for context from the 1985 NIV Study Bible by Zondervan Publishing House. A sincere thank you to both of these amazing organizations. Thank you to the excellent team at Amazon Publishing Portal.

Thank you to Tim House for providing a second set of eyes. A big, loving thank you to my wife, Shelley Stauffer, for her help and endless encouragement.

About Brian

Brian Stauffer thanks the LORD for blessing him with a wonderful family, initially his upbringing with loving parents and siblings, and now with his loving and encouraging wife, children, grandchildren and extended family. He gives God the glory for his career in corporate and ministry senior management as well as church leadership. He has been named All-American in both Triathlon and Biathlon (Duathlon); raced with three USA National Teams: Bicycling, Triathlon, and Duathlon; completed the Ironman Triathlon in Hawaii; and been the overall winner of more than 135 multi-sport endurance races.

Preface

I'm praying for you and that this devotional will be a daily inspiration for your athletic endeavors and will encourage you to look up these scriptures in their biblical context to draw closer and closer to our LORD every day.

To God be the glory as you go the extra mile – Matthew 5:41. You can do everything through Him who gives you strength – Philippians 4:13.

Brian

Table of Contents

Daily Scriptures

January 1
Isaiah 40:31
But those who hope in the Lord will renew their **strength.**
They will soar on wings like eagles; they will run and not grow
weary, they will walk and not be faint.

January 2
Isaiah 40:29
He gives **strength** to the weary and increases the power of the
weak.

January 3
2 Corinthians 6:3-4
We put no stumbling block in anyone's path, so that our
ministry will not be discredited. Rather, as servants of God we
commend ourselves in every way: in great **endurance**; in
troubles, hardships and distresses;

January 4
Deuteronomy 6:5
Love the Lord your God with all your heart and with all your
soul and with all your **strength.**

January 5
Judges 16:7
Samson answered her, "If anyone ties me with seven fresh
bowstrings that have not been dried, I'll become as **weak** as
any other man."

January 6
2 Samuel 22:33
It is God who arms me with **strength** and keeps my way secure.

January 7
2 Kings 23:25
Neither before nor after Josiah was there a king like him who turned to the Lord as he did—with all his heart and with all his soul and with all his **strength**, in accordance with all the Law of Moses.

January 8
1 Chronicles 16:11
Look to the Lord and his **strength**; seek his face always.

January 9
Matthew 14:28-30
"Lord, if it's you," Peter replied, "tell me to come to you on the **water**." "Come," he said. Then Peter got down out of the boat, **walked** on the water and came toward Jesus. But when he saw the wind, he was afraid and, beginning to sink, cried out, "Lord, save me!"

January 10
1 Chronicles 29:12
Wealth and honor come from you; you are the ruler of all things. In your hands are strength and power to exalt and give **strength** to all.

January 11
Nehemiah 8:10
Nehemiah said, "Go and enjoy choice food and sweet drinks, and send some to those who have nothing prepared. This day is holy to our Lord. Do not grieve, for the joy of the Lord is your **strength.**"

January 12
Matthew 5:41
If anyone forces you to go one **mile**, go with them two miles.

January 13
Psalms 28:7
The Lord is my **strength** and my shield; my heart trusts in him, and he helps me. My heart leaps for joy, and with my song I praise him.

January 14
Psalms 29:11
The Lord gives **strength** to his people; the Lord blesses his people with peace.

January 15
Psalms 16:18
No king is saved by the size of his army; no warrior escapes by his great **strength.** But the eyes of the Lord are on those who fear him, on those whose hope is in his unfailing love.

January 16
Psalms 46:1
God is our refuge and **strength,** an ever-present help in trouble.

January 17
Psalms 73:26
My flesh and my heart may fail, but God is the **strength** of my heart and my portion forever.

January 18
Hebrews 12:7
Endure hardship as discipline; God is treating you as his children. For what children are not disciplined by their father?

January 19
Psalms 105:4
Look to the Lord and his **strength;** seek his face always.

January 20
Psalms 118:14
The Lord is my **strength** and my defense; he has become my salvation.

January 21
Psalms 147:10-11
His pleasure is not in the **strength** of the horse, nor his delight in the **legs** of the warrior; the Lord delights in those who fear him, who put their hope in his unfailing love.

January 22
Ecclesiastes 9/17
The **quiet** words of the **wise** are more to be heeded than the shouts of a ruler of fools.

January 23
Isaiah 12:2
Surely God is my salvation; I will trust and not be afraid. The Lord, the Lord himself, is my **strength** and my defense; he has become my salvation."

January 24
Isaiah 31:1
Woe to those who go down to Egypt for help, who rely on horses, who trust in the multitude of their chariots and in the great **strength** of their horsemen, but do not look to the Holy One of Israel, or seek help from the Lord.

January 25
Jeremiah 9:23
This is what the Lord says: "Let not the wise **boast** of their wisdom or the strong boast of their **strength** or the rich boast of their riches, but let the one who boasts boast about this: that they have the understanding to know me, that I am the Lord, who exercises kindness, justice and righteousness on earth, for in these I delight," declares the Lord.

January 26
Habakkuk 3:19
The Sovereign Lord is my **strength;** he makes my feet like the feet of a deer, he enables me to tread on the heights.

January 27
Mark 12:30
Love the Lord your God with all your heart and with all your soul and with all your mind and with all your **strength.**

January 28
1 Corinthians 1:25
For the foolishness of God is wiser than human wisdom, and the weakness of God is stronger than human **strength.**

January 29
Philippians 4:13
I can do all this through him who gives me **strength.**

January 30
Hebrews 11:32-34
And what more shall I say? I do not have time to tell about Gideon, Barak, Samson and Jephthah, about David and Samuel and the prophets, who through faith conquered kingdoms, administered justice, and gained what was promised; who shut the mouths of lions, quenched the fury of the flames, and escaped the edge of the sword; whose **weakness** was turned to **strength;** and who became powerful in battle and routed foreign armies.

January 31
1 Peter 4:11
If anyone speaks, they should do so as one who speaks the very words of God. If anyone serves, they should do so with the **strength** God provides, so that in all things, God may be praised through Jesus Christ. To him be the glory and the power forever and ever. Amen.

February 1
Jeremiah 46:4
Take your positions with helmets on! Polish your spears, put on your **armor!**

February 2
2 Chronicles 16:9
For the eyes of the Lord range throughout the earth to **strengthen** those whose hearts are fully committed to him. You have done a foolish thing, and from now on you will be at war."

February 3
Psalms 119:28
My soul is weary with sorrow; **strengthen** me according to your word.

February 4
Isaiah 35:3-4
Strengthen the feeble hands, steady the knees that give way; say to those with fearful hearts, "Be **strong**, do not fear; your God will come, he will come with vengeance, with divine retribution. He will come to save you."

February 5
Ephesians 6:13-18
Therefore put on the full **armor** God, so that when the day of evil comes, you may be able to stand your ground, and after you have done everything, to stand. Stand firm then, with the belt of truth buckled around your waist, with the breastplate of righteous in place, and your feet fitted with the readiness that comes from the gospel of peace. In addition to all this, take up the shield of faith, with which you can extinguish all the flaming arrows of the evil one. Take the helmet of salvation and the sword of the spirit, which is the word of God. And pray in the Spirit on all occasions with all kinds of prayers and requests.

February 6
Titus 2:2
Teach the older men to be temperate, worthy of respect, self-controlled, and sound in faith, in love and in **endurance.**

February 7
1 Thessalonians 3:13
May he **strengthen** your hearts so that you will be blameless and holy in the presence of our God and Father when our Lord Jesus comes with all his holy ones.

February 8
2 Thessalonians 2:16-17
May our Lord Jesus Christ himself and God our Father, who loved us and by his grace gave us eternal **encouragement** and good hope, encourage your hearts and **strengthen** you in every good deed and word.

February 9
Hebrews 12:11-12
No discipline seems pleasant at the time, but painful. Later on, however, it produces a harvest of righteousness and peace for those who have been trained by it. Therefore, **strengthen** your feeble arms and weak knees.

February 10
Colossians 1:10-12
so that you may live a life worthy of the Lord and please him in every way: bearing fruit in every good work, growing in the knowledge of God, being **strengthened** with all **power** according to his glorious might so that you may have great **endurance** and **patience**, and giving joyful thanks to the Father, who has qualified you to share in the inheritance of his holy people in the kingdom of light.

February 11
Hebrews 13:9
Do not be carried away by all kinds of strange teachings. It is good for our hearts to be **strengthened** by grace, not by eating ceremonial foods, which is of no benefit to those who do so.

February 12
Deuteronomy 31:6
"Be **strong** and **courageous**. Do not be afraid or terrified because of them, for the Lord your God goes with you; he will never leave you nor forsake you."

February 13
Judges 5:21
March on, my soul; be **strong!**

February 14
2 Samuel 10:12
"Be **strong** and let us fight bravely for our people and the cities of our God. The Lord will do what is good in his sight."

February 15
1 Kings 2:2-3
"I am about to go the way of all the earth," he said. "So be **strong**, act like a man, and observe what the Lord your God requires: Walk in obedience to him, and keep his decrees and commands, his laws and regulations, as written in the Law of Moses. Do this so that you may prosper in all you do and wherever you go."

February 16
1 Chronicles 28:20
David also said to Solomon his son, "Be **strong and courageous**, and do the work. Do not be afraid or discouraged, for the Lord God, my God, is with you. He will not fail you or forsake you until all the work for the service of the temple of the Lord is finished."

February 17
2 Chronicles 32:6-7
He appointed military officers over the people and assembled them before him in the square at the city gate and encouraged them with these words: "Be **strong** and **courageous**. Do not be afraid or discouraged because of the king of Assyria and the vast army with him, for there is a greater **power** with us than with him."

February 18
Proverbs 31:17
She sets about her work vigorously; her arms are **strong** for her tasks.

February 19
Ecclesiastes 9:11
I have seen something else under the sun: The race is not to the **swift** or the battle to the **strong**, nor does food come to the **wise** or wealth to the brilliant or favor to the learned; but time and chance happen to them all.

10

February 20
Haggai 2:4
'But now be **strong,** Zerubbabel,' declares the Lord. 'Be **strong,** Joshua son of Jozadak, the high priest. Be **strong,** all you people of the land,' declares the Lord, 'and work. For I am with you,' declares the Lord Almighty.

February 21
Romans 15:1
We who are **strong** ought to bear with the failings of the weak and not to please ourselves.

February 22
1 Corinthians 1:8
He will also keep you **strong** to the end, so that you will be blameless on the day of our Lord Jesus Christ.

February 23
1 Corinthians 13:16
Be on your guard; stand firm in the faith; be **courageous**; be **strong**.

February 24
Ephesians 6:10
Finally, be **strong** in the Lord and in his mighty power.

February 25
2 Timothy 2:1
You then, my son, be **strong** in the grace that is in Christ Jesus.

February 26
1 Peter 5:10
And the God of all grace, who called you to his eternal glory in Christ, after you have suffered a little while, will himself restore you and make you **strong**, firm and steadfast.

February 27
Romans 15:4
For everything that was written in the past was written to teach us, so that through the **endurance** taught in the Scriptures and the **encouragement** they provide, we might have hope.

February 28
Romans 15:5-6
May the God who gives **endurance** and **encouragement** give you the same attitude of mind toward each other that Christ Jesus had, so that with one mind and one voice, you may glorify the God and Father of our Lord Jesus Christ.

February 29
Exodus 15:2
The lord is my **strength** and my defense; he has become my salvation. He is my God, and I will praise him, my father's God, and I will exalt him.

March 1
1 Thessalonians 1:3
We remember before our God and Father your work produced by faith, your labor prompted by love, and your **endurance** inspired by hope in our Lord Jesus Christ.

March 2
1 Timothy 6:11
But you, man of God, flee from all this, and pursue righteousness, godliness, faith, love, **endurance** and gentleness.

March 3
2 Timothy 3:10-11
You, however, know all about my teaching, my way of life, my purpose, faith, patience, love, **endurance,** persecutions, sufferings—

March 4
Ephesians 3:16-17
I pray that out of his glorious riches he may **strengthen** you with power through his Spirit in your inner being, so that Christ may dwell in your hearts through faith.

March 5
Revelation 13:10
This calls for patient **endurance** and faithfulness on the part of God's people.

March 6
1 Corinthians 4:12
We work hard with our own hands. When we are cursed, we bless; when we are persecuted, we **endure** it;

March 7
2 Corinthians 1:8-9
We do not want you to be uninformed, brothers and sisters, about the troubles we experienced in the province of Asia. We were under great pressure, far beyond our ability to **endure**, so that we despaired of life itself. Indeed, we felt we had received the sentence of death. But this happened that we might not rely on ourselves but on God, who raises the dead.

March 8
Psalms 18:1
I love you, Lord, my **strength**.

March 9
2 Timothy 2:10
Therefore, I **endure** everything for the sake of the elect, that they too may obtain the salvation that is in Christ Jesus, with eternal glory.

March 10
2 Timothy 2:12
If we **endure**, we will also reign with him.

March 11
2 Timothy 4:5
But you, keep your head in all situations, **endure** hardship, do the work of an evangelist, discharge all the duties of your ministry.

March 12
Psalms 84:5
Blessed are those whose **strength** is in you, whose hearts are set on pilgrimage.

March 13
1 Peter 2:20
But how is it to your credit if you receive a beating for doing wrong and **endure** it? But if you suffer for doing good and you **endure** it, this is commendable before God.

March 14
Psalms 132:1
Lord, remember David and all the hardships he **endured.**

March 15
Revelation 2:3
You have **persevered** and have **endured** hardships for my name, and have not grown weary.

March 16
Romans 13:12
The night is nearly over; The day is almost here. So let us put aside the deeds of darkness and put on the **armor** of light.

March 17
Psalms 23:4
Even though I walk through the darkest valley, I will **fear** no evil, for you are with me; your rod and your staff, they comfort me.

March 18
Psalms 46:2-3
Therefore we will not **fear**, though the earth give way and the mountains fall into the heart of the sea, though its waters roar and foam and the mountains quake with their surging.

March 19
Psalms 91:5-6
You will not **fear** the terror of night, nor the arrow that flies by day, nor the pestilence that stalks in the darkness, nor the plague that destroys at midday.

March 20
Psalms 111:10
The **fear** of the Lord is the beginning of **wisdom;** all who follow his precepts have good understanding. To him belongs eternal praise.

March 21
Psalms 118:4
Let those who **fear** the Lord say: "His love **endures** forever."

March 22
Proverbs 10:27
The **fear** of the Lord adds length to life, but the years of the wicked are cut short.

March 23
Proverbs 15:33
Wisdom's instruction is to **fear** the Lord, and **humility** comes before **honor.**

March 24
Proverbs 29:25
Fear of man will prove to be a snare, but whoever **trusts** in the Lord is kept safe.

March 25
Isaiah 41:10
So do not **fear**, for I am with you; do not be dismayed, for I am your God. I will **strengthen** you and help you; I will uphold you with my righteous right hand.

March 26
Isaiah 41:13
For I am the Lord your God who takes hold of your right hand and says to you, Do not **fear**; I will help you.

March 27
Isaiah 51:7
"Hear me, you who know what is right, you people who have taken my instruction to heart:
Do not **fear** the reproach of mere mortals or be terrified by their insults."

March 28
Isaiah 54:14
In righteousness you will be established:
Tyranny will be far from you; you will have nothing to **fear**.
Terror will be far removed; it will not come near you.

March 29
Jeremiah 17:7-8
"But blessed is the one who trusts in the Lord, whose **confidence** is in him. They will be like a tree planted by the water that sends out its roots by the stream. It does not **fear** when heat comes; its leaves are always green."

March 30
1 John 4:18
There is no **fear** in love. But perfect love drives out **fear**, because fear has to do with punishment. The one who **fears** is not made perfect in love.

March 31
Psalms 46:10
He says, "Be **still**, and know that I am God; I will be exalted among the nations, I will be exalted in the earth."

April 1
Psalms 34:4
I sought the LORD, and he answered me;   He delivered me from all my **fears**.

April 2
Proverbs 14:26
Whoever **fears** the LORD has a secure fortress, and for their children, it will be a refuge.

April 3
2 Corinthians 7:5-6
For when we came into Macedonia, we had no **rest**, but we were harassed at every turn—conflicts on the outside, **fears** within. But God, who comforts the downcast, comforted us...

April 4
Psalms 18:33
He makes my feet like the **feet** of a deer; he causes me to stand on the heights.

April 5
Proverbs 17:1
Better a dry crust with peace and quiet than a house full of **feasting,** with strife.

April 6
Psalms 40:2
He lifted me out of the slimy pit, out of the mud and mire; He set my **feet** on a rock and gave me a firm place to stand.

April 7
Psalms 56:13
For you have delivered me from death and my **feet** from stumbling, that I may walk before God in the light of life.

April 8
Psalms 66:8-9
Praise our God, all peoples, let the sound of his praise be heard; He has preserved our lives and kept our **feet** from slipping.

April 9
Psalms 73:2
But as for me, my **feet** had almost slipped; I had nearly lost my foothold.

April 10
Psalms 119:105
Your word is a lamp for my **feet**, a light on my path.

April 11
Proverbs 4:26
Give careful thought to the paths for your **feet** and be steadfast in all your ways.

April 12
Isaiah 52:7
How beautiful on the mountains are the **feet** of those who bring good news, who proclaim peace, who bring good tidings, who proclaim salvation, who say to Zion, "Your God reigns!"

April 13
1 Corinthians 12:21-23
The eye cannot say to the hand, "I don't need you!" And the head cannot say to the **feet**, "I don't need you!" On the contrary, those parts of the **body** that seem to be weaker are indispensable, and the parts that we think are less honorable we treat with special honor.

April 14
Luke 1:76-79
And you, my child, will be called a prophet of the Most High; For you will go on before the Lord to prepare the way for him, to give his people the knowledge of salvation through the forgiveness of their sins, because of the tender mercy of our God, by which the rising sun will come to us from heaven to shine on those living in darkness and in the shadow of death, to guide our **feet** into the path of peace.

April 15
Psalms 19:4-5
In the heavens, God has pitched a tent for the sun. It is like a bridegroom coming out of his chamber like a champion rejoicing to **run** his course.

April 16
Proverbs 4:12
When you walk, your steps will not be hampered; when you **run**, you will not stumble.

April 17
Proverbs 18:10
The name of the LORD is a fortified tower; the righteous **run** to it and are safe.

April 18
Isaiah 10:3
What will you do on the day of reckoning, when disaster comes from afar?
To whom will you **run** for help?
Where will you leave your riches?

April 19
Habakkuk 2:2
Then the LORD replied:
"Write down the revelation and make it plain on tablets so that a herald may **run** with it."

April 20
1 Corinthians 9:24
Do you not know that in a race all the runners **run**, but only one gets the prize? Run in such a way as to get the prize.

April 21
1 Corinthians 9:25
Everyone who competes in the games goes into strict **training.** They do it to get a crown that will not last, but we do it to get a crown that will last forever.

April 22
1 Corinthians 9:26
Therefore I do not **run** like someone **running** aimlessly; I do not fight like a boxer beating the air.

April 23
Galatians 2:2
I went in response to a revelation, and meeting privately with those esteemed as leaders, I presented to them the gospel that I preach among the Gentiles. I wanted to be sure I was not **running** and had not been **running** my **race** in vain.

April 24
Philippians 2:14-16
Do everything without grumbling or arguing so that you may become blameless and pure, "Children of God without fault in a warped and crooked generation." Then you will shine among them like stars in the sky as you hold firmly to the word of life. And then I will be able to boast on the day of Christ that I did not **run** or labor in vain.

April 25
Hebrews 12:1
Therefore, since we are surrounded by such a great cloud of witnesses, let us throw off everything that hinders and the sin that so easily entangles. And let us **run** with perseverance the **race** marked out for us.

April 26
Hebrews 12:2
Fixing our eyes on Jesus, the pioneer and perfecter of faith. For the joy set before him, he **endured** the cross, scorning its shame, and sat down at the right hand of the throne of God.

April 27
Exodus 31:15
For six days work is to be done, but the seventh day is a day of sabbath **rest**, holy to the LORD.

April 28
Exodus 33:14
The LORD replied, "My Presence will go with you, and I will give you **rest**."

April 29
Joshua 21:44
The LORD gave them **rest** on every side, just as he had sworn to their ancestors.

April 30
Psalms 16:9
Therefore, my heart is glad and my tongue rejoices; my body also will **rest** secure.

May 1
Psalms 62:5-6
Yes, my soul, find **rest** in God; My hope comes from him. Truly he is my rock and my salvation; He is my fortress I will not be shaken.

May 2
Psalms 91:1
Whoever dwells in the shelter of the Most High Will **rest** in the shadow of the Almighty.

May 3
Jeremiah 6:16
This is what the LORD says: "Stand at the crossroads and look; ask for the ancient paths, ask where the good way is, and **walk** in it, and you will find **rest** for your souls."

May 4
Matthew 11:28
"Come to me, all you who are weary and burdened, and I will give you **rest**."

May 5
Matthew 11:29-30
"Take my yoke upon you and learn from me, for I am gentle and humble in heart, and you will find **rest** for your souls. For my yoke is easy, and my burden is light."

May 6
John 20:3-9
So Peter and the other disciples started for the tomb. Both
were **running,** but the other disciple **outran** Peter and reached
the tomb first. He bent over and looked in at the strips of
linen lying there but did not go in. Then Simon Peter came
along behind him and went straight into the tomb. He saw the
strips of linen lying there, as well as the cloth that had been
wrapped around Jesus' head. The cloth was still lying in its
place, separate from the linen. Finally, the other disciple, who
had reached the tomb first, also went inside. He saw and
believed. (They still did not understand from Scripture that
Jesus had to rise from the dead).

May 7
John 21:7-8
Then the disciple whom Jesus loved said to Peter, "It is the
Lord!" As soon as Simon Peter heard him say, "It is the Lord,"
he wrapped his outer garment around him (for he had taken it
off) and **jumped into the water**. The other disciples followed
in the boat, towing the net full of fish, for they were not far
from shore, about a hundred yards.

May 8
Luke 15:18-20
"I will set out and go back to my father and say to him: Father,
I have sinned against heaven and against you. I am no longer
worthy to be called your son; make me like one of your hired
servants. So he got up and went to his father. But while he
was still a long way off, his father saw him and was filled with
compassion for him; he **ran** to his son, threw his arms around
him, and kissed him."

May 9
Isaiah 40:28
Do you not know?

Have you not heard?

The LORD is the everlasting God, the Creator of the ends of the earth.

He will not grow **tired or weary,** and his understanding no one can fathom.

May 10
Isaiah 50:4
The Sovereign LORD has given me a well-instructed tongue, to know the word that sustains the **weary.** He wakens me morning by morning, wakens my ear to listen like one being instructed.

May 11
Galatians 6:9
Let us not become **weary** of doing good, for at the proper time, we will reap a harvest if we do not give up.

May 12
Hebrews 12:1-3
Therefore, since we are surrounded by such a great cloud of witnesses, let us throw off everything that hinders and the sin that so easily entangles. And let us **run** with **perseverance** the race marked out for us, fixing our eyes on Jesus, the pioneer and perfecter of faith. For the joy set before him, he **endured** the cross, scorning its shame, and sat down at the right hand of the throne of God. Consider him who **endured** such opposition from sinners so that you will not grow **weary** and lose heart.

May 13
Matthew 15:5-6
May the God who gives **endurance** and **encouragement** give you the same attitude of mind toward each other that Christ Jesus had, so that with one mind and one voice you may glorify the God and Father of our Lord Jesus Christ.

May 14
1 Peter 3:4
Rather, it should be that of your inner self, the unfading beauty of a gentle and **quiet** spirit, which is of great worth in God's sight.

May 15
1 Samuel 2:3
"Do not keep talking so **proudly** or let your mouth speak such **arrogance**, for the LORD is a God who knows, and by him deeds are weighed."

May 16
2 Corinthians 12:8-9
Three times I pleaded with the Lord to take it away from me. But he said to me, "My grace is sufficient for you, for my **power** is made perfect in **weakness**." Therefore, I will boast all the more gladly about my **weaknesses**, so that Christ's **power** may rest on me.

May 17
2 Corinthians 12:10
That is why, for Christ's sake, I delight in **weaknesses,** in insults, in hardships, in persecutions, in difficulties. For when I am **weak**, then I am **strong.**

May 18
Hebrews 12:12
Therefore, **strengthen** your feeble arms and **weak** knees.

May 19
Romans 8:26
In the same way, the Spirit helps us in our **weakness**. We do not know what we ought to pray for, but the Spirit himself intercedes for us through wordless groans.

May 20
2 Corinthians 11:30
If I must **boast,** I will **boast** of the things that show my **weakness**.

May 21
2 Corinthians 12:5
I will **boast** about a man like that, but I will not **boast** about myself except about my **weaknesses.**

May 22
Hebrews 4:15-16
For we do not have a high priest who is unable to empathize with our **weaknesses**, but we have one who has been tempted in every way, just as we are—yet he did not sin. Let us then approach God's throne of grace with **confidence** so that we may receive mercy and find grace to help us in our time of need.

May 23
Deuteronomy 8:17
You may say to yourself, "My **power** and the **strength** of my hands have produced this wealth for me." But remember the LORD your God, for it is he who gives you the ability to produce wealth and so confirms his covenant, which he swore to your ancestors, as it is today.

May 24
1 Samuel 10:6-7
The Spirit of the LORD will come upon you in **power**, and you will prophesy with them; and you will be changed into a different person. Once these signs are fulfilled, do whatever your hand finds to do, for God is with you.

May 25
1 Samuel 16:13
So Samuel took the horn of oil and anointed him in the presence of his brothers, and from that day on the Spirit of the LORD came **powerfully** upon David. Samuel then went to Ramah.

May 26
Proverbs 24:5
The wise prevail through great **power**, and those who have knowledge muster their **strength.**

May 27
Zechariah 4:6
So he said to me, "This is the word of the LORD to Zerubbabel: 'Not by **might** nor by **power,** but by my **Spirit**,' says the LORD Almighty."

May 28
Luke 24:49
"I am going to send you what my Father has promised, but stay in the city until you have been clothed with **power** from on high."

May 29
Acts 1:8
"But you will receive **power** when the Holy Spirit comes on you; and you will be my witnesses in Jerusalem, and in all Judea and Samaria, and to the ends of the earth."

May 30
Acts 4:33
With great **power,** the apostles continued to testify to the resurrection of the Lord Jesus. And God's grace was so **powerfully** at work in them all.

May 31
Romans 15:13
May the God of hope fill you with all joy and peace as you trust in him so that you may overflow with hope by the **power** of the Holy **Spirit**.

June 1
1 Corinthians 2:4-5
My message and my preaching were not with wise and persuasive words, but with a demonstration of the Spirit's **power**, so that your faith might not rest on human wisdom, but on God's **power.**

June 2

2 Corinthians 10:4

The weapons we fight with are not the weapons of the world. On the contrary, they have the divine **power** to demolish strongholds.

June 3

Ephesians 1:18-21

I pray that the eyes of your heart may be enlightened in order that you may know the hope to which he has called you, the riches of his glorious inheritance in his holy people, and his incomparably great **power** for us who believe. That power is the same as the mighty **strength** he exerted when he raised Christ from the dead and seated him at his right hand in the heavenly realms, far above all rule and authority, **power** and dominion, and every name that is invoked, not only in the present age but also in the one to come.

June 4

Psalms 5:5

The **arrogant** cannot stand in your presence. You hate all who do wrong.

June 5

Ephesians 3:20-21

Now to him who is able to do immeasurably more than all we ask or imagine, according to his **power** that is at work within us, to him be glory in the church and in Christ Jesus throughout all generations, forever and ever! Amen.

June 6
1 Thessalonians 1:4-5
For we know, brothers and sisters loved by God, that he has chosen you, because our gospel came to you not simply with words but also with **power**, with the Holy Spirit and deep conviction.

June 7
2 Timothy 1:7
For the Spirit God gave us does not make us timid but gives us **power**, love, and **self-discipline**.

June 8
2 Peter 1:3
His divine **power** has given us everything we need for a godly life through our knowledge of him, who called us by his own glory and goodness.

June 9
2 Chronicles 27:6
Jotham grew **powerful** because he walked steadfastly before the LORD his God.

June 10
James 5:16
Therefore confess your sins to each other and pray for each other so that you may be healed. The prayer of a righteous person is **powerful** and effective.

June 11
Romans 5:6
You see, at just the right time, when we were still **powerless**, Christ died for the ungodly.

June 12
Acts 20:24
However, I consider my life worth nothing to me; my only aim is to finish the **race** and complete the task the Lord Jesus has given me—the task of testifying to the good news of God's grace.

June 13
Galatians 5:7
You were **running** a good **race**. Who cut in on you to keep you from obeying the truth?

June 14
2 Timothy 4:7
I have fought the good fight, I have finished the **race**, I have kept the faith.

June 15
2 Timothy 2:5
Similarly, anyone who **competes** as an **athlete** does not receive the victor's crown except by competing according to the rules.

June 16
James 3:13
Who is wise and understanding among you? Let them show it by their good life, by deeds done in the **humility** that comes from wisdom.

June 17
Psalms 18:32
It is God who arms me with **strength** and keeps my way secure.

June 18
Psalms 21:5
Through the **victories** you gave, his glory is great; You have
bestowed on him splendor and majesty.

June 19
Psalms 21:1
The king rejoices in your **strength**, LORD.
How great is his joy in the **victories** you give!

June 20
Psalms 20:5
May we shout for joy over your **victory** and lift up our
banners in the name of our God.

June 21
2 Samuel 8:6
The LORD gave David **victory** wherever he went.

June 22
Psalms 44:6-8
I put no trust in my bow, my sword does not bring me **victory**;
but you give us **victory** over our enemies, You put our
adversaries to shame.
In God, we make our boast all day long, and we will praise
your name forever.

June 23
Psalms 60:12
With God, we will gain the **victory,** And he will trample down
our enemies.

June 24
1 Corinthians 15:57
But thanks be to God! He gives us the **victory** through our Lord Jesus Christ.

June 25
Proverbs 25:27
Like a city whose walls are broken through is a person who lacks **self-control.**

June 26
Galatians 5:22
But the fruit of the Spirit is love, joy, peace, patience, kindness, goodness, faithfulness gentleness, and **self-control.**

June 27
2 Peter 1:5-7
For this very reason, make every effort to add to your faith goodness; and to goodness, knowledge; and to knowledge, **self-control**; and to **self-control**, perseverance; and to perseverance, godliness; and to godliness, mutual affection; and to mutual affection, love.

June 28
1 Thessalonians 5:8
But since we belong to the day, let us be **self-controlled,** putting on faith and love as a breastplate and the hope of salvation as a helmet.

June 29
Titus 1:8
Rather, he must be hospitable, one who loves what is good, who is **self-controlled**, upright, holy, and disciplined.

June 30
Titus 2:6
Similarly, encourage the young men to be **self-controlled.**

July 1
1 Peter 1:13
Therefore, prepare your minds for action; be **self-controlled**; set your hope fully on the grace to be given you when Christ Jesus is revealed.

July 2
1 Peter 4:7
The end of all things is near. Therefore be clear minded and **self-controlled** so you can pray.

July 3
1 Peter 5:8
Be **self-controlled** and alert.

July 4
Romans 5:3-4
Not only so, but we also glory in our sufferings because we know that suffering produces **perseverance**; perseverance, character; and character, hope.

July 5
James 1:2-4
Consider it pure joy, my brothers and sisters, whenever you face trials of many kinds because you know that the testing of your faith produces **perseverance**. Let perseverance finish its work so that you may be mature and complete, not lacking anything.

July 6
Philippians 3:13-14
Brothers and sisters, I do not consider myself yet to have taken hold of it. But one thing I do: Forgetting what is behind and **straining** toward what is ahead, I press on toward the **goal** to win the prize for which God has called me heavenward in Christ Jesus.

July 7
James 5:11
As you know, we count as blessed those who have **persevered**. You have heard of Job's perseverance and have seen what the Lord finally brought about. The Lord is full of compassion and mercy.

July 8
Revelation 2:2
I know your deeds, your hard work, and your **perseverance**. I know that you cannot tolerate wicked people, that you have tested those who claim to be apostles but are not, and have found them false.

July 9
Revelation 2:19
I know your deeds, your love and faith, your service and **perseverance**, and that you are now doing more than you did at first.

July 10
1 Timothy 4:16
Watch your life and doctrine closely. **Persevere** in them, because if you do, you will save both yourself and your hearers.

July 11
Hebrews 10:36
You need to **persevere** so that when you have done the will of God, you will receive what he has promised.

July 12
Hebrews 11:27
By faith he left Egypt, not fearing the king's anger; he **persevered** because he saw him who is invisible.

July 13
1 Corinthians 13:7
It [love] always protects, always trusts, always hopes, always **perseveres**.

July 14
Ezekiel 36:25-26
I will sprinkle clean water on you, and you will be clean; I will cleanse you from all your impurities and from all your idols. I will give you a new heart and put a new spirit in you; I will remove from you your heart of stone and give you a heart of **flesh**.

July 15
Luke 8:15
But the seed on good soil stands for those with a noble and good heart, who hear the word, retain it, and by **persevering** produce a crop.

July 16
1 Corinthians 10:31
So whether you eat or drink or whatever you do, do it all for the **glory** of God.

July 17
1 Peter 1:24-5
For, "All people are like grass, and all their **glory** is like the flowers of the field; the grass withers and the flowers fall, but the word of the Lord endures forever."

July 18
1 Peter 5:4
And when the Chief Shepherd appears, you will receive the crown of **glory** that will never fade away.

July 19
1 Peter 5:5
All of you, clothe yourselves with **humility** toward one another, because, "God opposes the **proud** but shows favor to the **humble**."

July 20
1 Peter 5:6
Humble yourselves, therefore, under God's mighty hand, that he may lift you up in due time.

July 21
Psalms 37:23-24
The LORD makes firm the **steps** of the one who delights in him; though he may **stumble,** he will not fall, for the LORD upholds him with his hand.

July 22
Proverbs 14:15
The simple believe anything, but the prudent give thought to their **steps.**

July 23
Proverbs 16:9
In their hearts, humans plan their **course**, but the LORD establishes their **steps.**

July 24
Proverbs 20:24
A person's **steps** are directed by the LORD.
How, then, can anyone understand their own way?

July 25
Proverbs 15:22
Plans fail for lack of counsel, but with many advisers, they **succeed.**

July 26
Proverbs 16:3
Commit to the LORD whatever you do, and he will establish your **plans.**

July 27
Proverbs 19:21
Many are the **plans** in a person's heart, but it is the LORD's purpose that prevails.

July 28
Proverbs 20:18
Plans are established by seeking advice; so if you wage war, obtain guidance.

July 29
Isaiah 32:8
But the noble make noble **plans**, and by noble deeds, they stand.

July 30
2 Corinthians 1:17
Was I fickle when I intended to do this? Or do I make my **plans** in a worldly manner so that in the same breath, I say both "Yes, yes" and "No, no"?

July 31
Galatians 3:3
Are you so foolish? After beginning with the Spirit, are you now trying to attain your **goal** by human effort?

August 1
2 Kings 18:19
"This is what the great king, the king of Assyria, says: On what are you basing this **confidence** of yours?"

August 2
2 Chronicles 32:10
"This is what Sennacherib king of Assyria says: On what are you basing your **confidence**, that you remain in Jerusalem under siege?"

August 3
Job 4:6
Should not your piety be your **confidence** and your blameless
ways your hope?

August 4
Psalms 71:5
For you have been my hope, Sovereign LORD, my **confidence**
since my youth.

August 5
Proverbs 3:25-26
Have no fear of sudden disaster or of the ruin that overtakes
the wicked, for the LORD will be your **confidence** and will
keep your foot from being snared.

August 6
Isaiah 32:17
The fruit of that righteousness will be peace; its effect will be
quietness and **confidence** forever.

August 7
Romans 11:20
Granted. But they were broken off because of unbelief, and
you stand by faith. Do not be **arrogant**, but tremble.

August 8
2 Corinthians 3:4-5
Such **confidence** we have through Christ before God. Not that
we are competent in ourselves to claim anything for ourselves,
but our competence comes from God.

August 9
1 Corinthians 1:19
Do you not know that your **bodies** are temples of the Holy Spirit, who is in you, whom you have received from God?

August 10
1 Timothy 4:8
For physical **training** is of some value, but godliness has value for all things, holding promise for both the present life and the life to come.

August 11
Philippians 3:3-4
For it is we who are the circumcision, we who serve God by his Spirit, who boast in Christ Jesus, and who put no **confidence** in the flesh—though I myself have reasons for such confidence.

August 12
Hebrews 3:14
We have come to share in Christ if we hold firmly to the end the **confidence** we had at first.

August 13
Hebrews 10:35
So do not throw away your **confidence**; it will be richly rewarded.

August 14
1 John 3:21
Dear friends, if our hearts do not condemn us, we have **confidence** before God and receive from him anything we ask, because we obey his commands and do what pleases him.

August 15
1 John 5:14-15
This is the **confidence** we have in approaching God: that if we ask anything according to his will, he hears us. And if we know that he hears us—whatever we ask—we know that we have what we asked of him.

August 16
Psalms 27:3
Though an army besiege me, my heart will not fear; though war break out against me, even then, I will be **confident.**

August 17
Luke 14:11
All those who exalt themselves will be humbled, and those who **humble** themselves will be exalted."

August 18
Psalms 27:13
I remain **confident** of this: I will see the goodness of the LORD in the land of the living.

August 19
Luke 18:9
To some who were **confident** of their own righteousness and looked down on everyone else, Jesus told this parable: [The Pharisee and the tax collector]... "For everyone who exalts himself will be humbled, and he who humbles himself will be exalted."

August 20
2 Corinthians 5:6
Therefore we are always **confident** and know that as long as we are at home in the body we are away from the Lord.

August 21
2 Corinthians 5:8
We are **confident,** I say, and would prefer to be away from the body and at home with the Lord.

August 22
Philippians 1:6
...being **confident** of this, that he who began a good work in you will carry it on to completion until the day of Christ Jesus.

August 23
3 John 2
Dear friend, I pray that you may enjoy good **health** and that all may go well with you, even as your soul is getting along well.

August 24
1 Samuel 25:6
Say to him: "Long life to you! Good **health** to you and your household! And good health to all that is yours!"

August 25
Proverbs 31:7-8
Do not be wise in your own eyes; fear the LORD and shun evil. This will bring **health** to your body and nourishment to your bones.

August 26
Proverbs 4:20-22
My son, pay attention to what I say; turn your ear to my words. Do not let them out of your sight, keep them within your heart; for they are life to those who find them and **health** to one's whole body

August 27
Psalms 119:32
I **run** in the path of your commands, for you have broadened my understanding.

August 28
Proverbs 15:30
Light in a messenger's eyes brings joy to the heart, and good news gives **health** to the bones.

August 29
Isaiah 38:16
Lord, by such things people live; and my spirit finds life in them too. You restored me to **health** and let me live.

August 30
Jeremiah 3:6
"Nevertheless, I will bring **health** and healing to it; I will heal my people and will let them enjoy abundant peace and security."

August 31
Daniel 1:15
At the end of the ten days, they looked **healthier** and better nourished than any of the young men who ate the royal food.

September 1
Mathew 9:12-13
On hearing this, Jesus said, "It is not the **healthy** who need a doctor, but the sick. But go and learn what this means: 'I desire mercy, not sacrifice. For I have not come to call the righteous, but sinners.'"

September 2
Judges 14:6
The Spirit of the LORD came **powerfully** upon him [Sampson] so that he tore the lion apart with his bare hands as he might have torn a young goat. But he told neither his father nor his mother what he had done.

September 3
Judges 15:14
As he approached Lehi, the Philistines came toward him shouting. The Spirit of the LORD came **powerfully** upon him. The ropes on his arms became like charred flax, and the bindings dropped from his hands.

September 4
Judges15:19
Then God opened up the hollow place in Lehi, and water came out of it. When Samson drank, his **strength** returned, and he revived. So, the spring was called En Hakkore, and it is still in Lehi.

September 5
Judges 16:28-30
Then Samson prayed to the LORD, "Sovereign LORD, remember me. Please, God, **strengthen** me just once more, and let me with one blow get revenge on the Philistines for my two eyes." Then Samson reached toward the two central pillars on which the temple stood. Bracing himself against them, his right hand on the one and his left hand on the other, Samson said, "Let me die with the Philistines!" Then he pushed with all his might, and down came the temple on the rulers and all the people in it.

September 6
Psalms 116:165
Great peace have those who love your law, and nothing can make them **stumble.**

September 7
Proverbs 3:23
Then you will go on your way in safety, and your foot will not **stumble.**

September 8
Jeremiah 13:16
Give glory to the LORD your God before he brings the darkness, before your feet **stumble** on the darkening hills.

September 9
Hosea 14:9
Who is wise? Let them realize these things.
Who is discerning? Let them understand.
The ways of the LORD are right; the righteous walk in them, but the rebellious **stumble** in them.

September 10
John 11:9-10
Jesus answered, "Are there not twelve hours of daylight? Anyone who walks in the daytime will not **stumble,** for they see by this world's light. It is when a person walks at night that they stumble, for they have no light.

September 11
Romans 9:33
As it is written: "See, I lay in Zion a stone that causes people to **stumble** and a rock that makes them fall, and the one who believes in him will never be put to shame."

September 12
Romans 14:20-22
All food is clean, but it is wrong for a person to eat anything that causes someone else to **stumble**. It is better not to eat meat drink wine or to do anything else that will cause your brother or sister to fall. So whatever you believe about these things keep between yourself and God.

September 13
James 3:2
We all **stumble** in many ways.

September 14
1 Peter 2:7-8
Now to you who believe, this stone is precious. But to those who do not believe, "The stone the builders rejected has become the cornerstone," and, "A stone that causes people to **stumble** and a rock that makes them fall."

September 15
Job 22:21
"Submit to God and be at **peace** with him; in this way prosperity will come to you.

September 16
1 John 2:10
Anyone who loves their brother and sister lives in the light, and there is nothing in them to make them **stumble.**

September 17
Proverbs 24:17-18
Do not gloat when your enemy falls; when they **stumble,** do not let your heart rejoice, or the LORD will see and disapprove and turn his wrath away from them.

September 18
James 2:10
For whoever keeps the whole law and yet **stumbles** at just one point is guilty of breaking all of it.

September 19
Romans 9:32
Why not? Because they pursued it not by faith but as if it were by works. They **stumbled** over the stumbling stone.

September 20
Romans 14:13
Therefore let us stop passing judgment on one another. Instead, make up your mind not to put any **stumbling** block or obstacle in the way of a brother or sister.

September 21
1 Corinthians 8:9
Be careful, however, that the exercise of your rights does not become a **stumbling** block to the weak.

September 22
2 Corinthians 6:3
We put no **stumbling** block in anyone's path so that our ministry will not be discredited.

September 23
Numbers 12:3
(Now Moses was a very **humble** man, more humble than anyone else on the face of the earth.)

September 24
Psalms 18:27
You save the **humble** but bring low those whose eyes are haughty.

September 25
Psalms 25:9
He guides the **humble** in what is right and teaches them his way.

September 26
Psalms 129:4
For the LORD takes delight in his people; he crowns the **humble** with victory.

September 27
Proverbs 3:34
He mocks proud mockers but shows favor to the **humble** and oppressed.

September 28
Isaiah 66:2
"These are the ones I look on with favor: those who are **humble** and contrite in spirit, and who tremble at my word.

September 29
Ephesians 4:2
Be completely **humble** and gentle; be patient, bearing with one another in love.

September 30
James 4:6
But he gives us more grace. That is why Scripture says: "God opposes the proud but shows favor to the **humble**."

October 1
James 4:10
Humble yourselves before the Lord, and he will lift you up.

October 2
Proverbs 8:13
When pride comes, then comes disgrace, but with **humility** comes wisdom.

October 3
Proverbs 13:10
Where there is strife, there is **pride**, but wisdom is found in those who take advice.

October 4
Proverbs 16:18
Pride goes before destruction, a haughty spirit before a fall.

October 5
Proverbs 29:23
Pride brings a person low, but the lowly in spirit gain honor.

October 6
Galatians 6:4-5
Each one should test their own actions. Then they can take **pride** in themselves alone, without comparing themselves to someone else, for each one should carry their own load.

October 7
Romans 12:1
Therefore, I urge you, brothers and sisters, in view of God's mercy, to offer your **bodies** as a living sacrifice, holy and pleasing to God—this is your true and proper worship.

October 8
1 Corinthians 6:15
Do you not know that your **bodies** are members of Christ himself?

October 9
Matthew 26:41
"Watch and pray so that you will not fall into temptation. The spirit is willing, but the **body** is **weak**."

October 10
Romans 6:13
Do not offer any part of the **body** to sin as an instrument of wickedness, but rather offer yourselves to God as those who have been brought from death to life; and offer the parts of your body to him as instruments of righteousness.

October 11
1 Corinthians 6:19-20
You are not your own; you were bought at a price. Therefore honor God with your **bodies.**

October 12
1 Corinthians 15:44
If there is a natural **body,** there is also a spiritual body.

October 13
Ephesians 5:29-30
After all, no one ever hated their own **body,** but they feed and care for their body, just as Christ does the church—for we are members of his body.

October 14
Philippians 1:20
I eagerly expect and hope that I will in no way be ashamed but will have sufficient courage so that now, as always, Christ will be exalted in my **body**, whether by life or by death.

October 15
James 2:15-17
Suppose a brother or a sister is without clothes and daily food. If one of you says to them, "Go in peace; keep warm and well fed," but does nothing about their **physical** needs, what good is it? In the same way, faith by itself, if it is not accompanied by action, is dead.

October 16
1 Timothy 4:7
Have nothing to do with godless myths and old wives' tales; rather, **train** yourself to be godly.

October 17
2 Chronicles 32:8
"With him is only the arm of **flesh**, but with us is the LORD our God to help us and to fight our battles."

October 18
Luke 6:40
The student is not above the teacher, but everyone who is fully **trained** will be like their teacher.

October 19
Hebrews 12:11
No discipline seems pleasant at the time but painful. Later on, however, it produces a harvest of righteousness and peace for those who have been **trained** by it.

October 20
Proverbs 19:15
Laziness brings on deep sleep, and the shiftless go hungry.

October 21
Proverbs 10:4
Lazy hands make for poverty, but diligent hands bring wealth.

October 22
Ecclesiastes 10:18
Through **laziness**, the rafters sag; because of idle hands, the house leaks.

October 23
Hebrews 6:12
We do not want you to become **lazy** but to imitate those who, through faith and patience, inherit what has been promised.

October 24
Genesis 39:23
The warden paid no attention to anything under Joseph's care because the LORD was with Joseph and gave him **success** in whatever he did.

October 25
1 Samuel 18:14
In everything he did, he had great **success**, because the LORD was with him.

October 26
1 Chronicles 12:18
Success, success to you, and success to those who help you, for your God will help you."

October 27
1 Chronicles 22:13
Then you will have **success** if you are careful to observe the decrees and laws that the LORD gave Moses for Israel. Be **strong** and **courageous**. Do not be afraid or discouraged.

October 28
2 Chronicles 26:5
As long as he sought the LORD, God gave him **success.**

October 29
Ecclesiastes 10:10
If the ax is dull and its edge unsharpened, more **strength** is needed, but skill will bring **success**.

October 30
Joshua 1:7
Be **strong** and very **courageous.** Be careful to obey all the law my servant Moses gave you; do not turn from it to the right or to the left, that you may be **successful** wherever you go.

October 31
2 Kings 18:6-7
He held fast to the LORD and did not stop following him; he kept the commands the LORD had given Moses. And the LORD was with him; he was **successful** in whatever he undertook.

November 1
2 Chronicles 20:20
Early in the morning they left for the Desert of Tekoa. As they set out, Jehoshaphat stood and said, "Listen to me, Judah and people of Jerusalem! Have faith in the LORD your God, and you will be upheld; have faith in his prophets, and you will be **successful.**"

November 2
1 Peter 3:17
For it is better, if it is God's will, to **suffer** for doing good than for doing evil.

November 3
1 Peter 4:16
However, if you **suffer** as a Christian, do not be ashamed, but praise God that you bear that name.

November 4
1 Peter 4:1
Therefore, since Christ suffered in his body, arm yourselves also with the same attitude, because whoever **suffers** in the body is done with sin.

November 5
Job 36:15
But those who **suffer** he delivers in their suffering; he speaks to them in their affliction.

November 6
Psalm 22:24
For he has not despised or scorned the **suffering** of the afflicted one; he has not hidden his face from him but has listened to his cry for help.

November 7
1 Peter 4:12
Dear friends, do not be surprised at the painful trial you are **suffering,** as though something strange was happening to you. But rejoice that you participate in the sufferings of Christ, so that you may be overjoyed when his glory is revealed.

November 8
James 1:2
Consider it pure joy, my brothers and sisters, whenever you face trials of many kinds, [3] because you know that the testing of your faith produces **perseverance.**

November 9
Psalm 139:14-16
I praise you because I am fearfully and wonderfully made; your works are wonderful, I know that full well.
My frame was not hidden from you when I was made in the secret place, when I was woven together in the depths of the earth.
Your eyes saw my unformed **body;** all the days ordained for me were written in your book before one of them came to be.

November 10
Colossians 1:29
To this end I labor, **struggling** with all his **energy,** which so powerfully works in me.

November 11
Romans 8:18
I consider that our present **sufferings** are not worth comparing with the glory that will be revealed in us.

November 12
Proverbs 13:20
Walk with the wise and become **wise,** for a companion of fools suffers harm.

November 13
1 Corinthians 12:24-26
But God has put the **body** together, giving greater honor to the parts that lacked it, so that there should be no division in the body, but that its parts should have equal concern for each other. If one part suffers, every part suffers with it; if one part is honored, every part rejoices with it.

November 14
1 Thessalonians 2:19
For what is our hope, our joy, or the **crown** in which we will glory in the presence of our Lord Jesus when he comes?

November 15
James 1:12
Blessed is the one who **perseveres** under trial because, having stood the test, that person will receive the **crown** of life that the Lord has promised to those who love him.

November 16
Revelation 2:10
Do not be afraid of what you are about to **suffer.** I tell you, the devil will put some of you in prison to test you, and you will suffer persecution for ten days. Be faithful, even to the point of death, and I will give you life as your **victor's crown.**

November 17
Proverbs 14:18
The simple inherit folly, but the prudent are **crowned** with **knowledge.**

November 18
Psalms 103:2-5
Praise the LORD, my soul, and forget not all his benefits— who forgives all your sins and heals all your diseases, who redeems your life from the pit and **crowns** you with love and compassion, who satisfies your desires with good things so that your youth is renewed like the eagle's.

November 19
Psalms 31:23
Love the LORD and all his faithful people!
The LORD preserves those who are true to him, but the **proud** he pays back in full.

November 20
Psalms 101:5
Whoever slanders their neighbor in secret, I will put to silence; whoever has haughty eyes and a **proud** heart, I will not tolerate it.

November 21
Psalms 139:13
For you **created** my inmost being; you knit me together in my mother's womb.

November 22
Psalms 138:6
Though the LORD is exalted, he looks kindly on the lowly; but the **proud,** he knows from afar.

November 23
Proverbs 16:5
The LORD detests all the **proud** of heart. Be sure of this: They will not go unpunished.

November 24
Proverbs 16:19
Better to be lowly in spirit along with the oppressed than to share plunder with the **proud.**

November 25
Proverbs 18:12
Before a downfall, the heart is **proud**, but **humility** comes before honor.

November 26
Romans 12:16
Live in harmony with one another. Do not be **proud**, but be willing to associate with people of low position. Do not be conceited.

November 27
Deuteronomy 5:33
Walk in obedience to all that the LORD your God has commanded you, so that you may live and **prosper** and prolong your days in the land that you will possess.

November 28
Deuteronomy 29:9
Carefully follow the terms of this covenant, so that you may **prosper** in everything you do.

November 29
Ephesians 6:12
For our struggle is not against **flesh** and blood, but against the rulers, against the authorities, against the powers of this dark world and against the spiritual forces of evil in the heavenly realms.

November 30
Proverbs 11:10
When the righteous **prosper**, the city rejoices; when the wicked perish, there are shouts of joy.

December 1
Proverbs 11:25
A generous person will **prosper;** whoever refreshes others will be refreshed.

December 2
Proverbs 28:25
The greedy stir up conflict, but those who trust in the LORD will **prosper.**

December 3
Genesis 39:2
The LORD was with Joseph so that he **prospered**, and he lived in the house of his Egyptian master.

December 4
2 Chronicles 14:7
"Let us build up these towns," he said to Judah, "and put walls around them, with towers, gates, and bars. The land is still ours because we have sought the LORD our God; we sought him, and he has given us rest on every side." So they built and **prospered.**

December 5
2 Chronicles 31:21
In everything that he undertook in the service of God's temple and in obedience to the law and the commands, he sought his God and worked wholeheartedly. And so he **prospered.**

December 6
Deuteronomy 28:9-11
The LORD will establish you as his holy people, as he promised you on oath if you keep the commands of the LORD your God and walk in obedience to him. Then all the people on earth will see that you are called by the name of the LORD, and they will fear you. The LORD will grant you abundant **prosperity**—

December 7
Job 36:11
If they obey and serve him, they will spend the rest of their days in **prosperity** and their years in contentment.

December 8
Psalms 122:9
For the sake of the house of the LORD our God, I will seek your **prosperity.**

December 9
Psalms 128:1-2
Blessed are all who fear the LORD, who walk in obedience to him.
You will eat the fruit of your labor; blessings and **prosperity** will be yours.

December 10
Proverbs 3:1-2
My son, do not forget my teaching, but keep my commands in your heart, for they will prolong your life for many years and bring you peace and **prosperity.**

December 11
Proverbs 13:21
Misfortune pursues the sinner, but **prosperity** is the reward of the righteous.

December 12
Deuteronomy 30:8-9
You will again obey the LORD and follow all his commands I am giving you today. Then the LORD your God will make you most **prosperous** in all the work of your hands and in the fruit of your womb, the young of your livestock, and the crops of your land.

December 13
Joshua 1:8
Keep this Book of the Law always on your lips; meditate on it day and night, so that you may be careful to do everything written in it. Then you will be **prosperous** and successful.

December 14
Job 42:10
After Job had prayed for his friends, the LORD made him **prosperous** again and gave him twice as much as he had before.

December 15
Psalms 1:1-3
Blessed is the one who does not walk in step with the wicked or stand in the way that sinners take or sit in the company of mockers, but whose delight is in the law of the LORD, and who meditates on his law day and night.
That person is like a tree planted by streams of water, which yields its fruit in season and whose leaf does not wither— whatever they do **prospers.**

December 16
Proverbs 16:20
Whoever gives heed to instruction **prospers,** and blessed is the one who trusts in the LORD.

December 17
Proverbs 19:8
The one who gets wisdom loves life; The one who cherishes understanding will soon **prosper.**

December 18
Matthew 23:12
For those who exalt themselves will be humbled, and those who **humble** themselves will be exalted.

December 19
Matthew 18:4
Therefore, whoever **humbles** himself like this child is the greatest in the kingdom of heaven.

December 20
Proverbs 22:4
Humility is the fear of the LORD; its wages are riches and honor and life.

December 21
Philippians 2:3-4
Do nothing out of selfish ambition or vain conceit. Rather, in **humility** value others above yourselves, not looking to your own interests but each of you to the interests of the others.

December 22
Colossians 3:12
Therefore, as God's chosen people, holy and dearly loved, clothe yourselves with compassion, kindness, **humility**, gentleness, and patience.

December 23
Titus 3:1-2
Remind the people to be subject to rulers and authorities, to be obedient, to be ready to do whatever is good, to slander no one, to be peaceable and considerate, and to show true **humility** toward everyone.

December 24
Isaiah 7:14
Therefore the LORD himself will give you a sign: The virgin will conceive and give birth to a son, and will call him **Immanuel**. [Which means God with us.]

December 25
Luke 2:8-11
And there were shepherds living out in the fields nearby, keeping watch over their flocks at night. An angel of the Lord appeared to them, and the **glory** of the Lord shone around them, and they were terrified. But the angel said to them, "Do not be afraid. I bring you good news that will cause great joy for all the people. Today in the town of David a **Savior** has been born to you; he is the Messiah, the Lord.

December 26
Proverbs 16:7
When the Lord takes pleasure in anyone's way, he causes their enemies to make **peace** with them.

December 27
Matthew 11:19
"But **wisdom** is proved right by her deeds."

December 28
James 1:4
Let **perseverance** finish its work so that you may be mature and complete, not lacking anything.

December 29
Genesis 2:2-3
By the seventh day God had finished the work he had been doing; so on the seventh day he **rested** from all his work. Then God blessed the seventh day and made it holy, because on it he rested from all the work of creating that he had done.

December 30
Proverbs 3:13-14
Blessed are those who find **wisdom,** those who gain understanding, for she is more profitable than silver and yields better returns than gold.

December 31
James 1:5
If any of you lacks **wisdom,** you should ask God, who gives generously to all without finding fault, and it will be given to you.

Bonus Encouragement (BE)

One
Psalms 42:1
As the deer pants for streams of **water,** so my soul pants for you, my God.

Two
Isaiah 12:3
With joy, you will draw **water** from the wells of salvation.

Three
Isaiah 32:2
Each one will be like a shelter from the wind and a refuge from the storm, like streams of **water** in the desert and the shadow of a great rock in a thirsty land.

Four
Isaiah 49:10
They will neither hunger nor thirst, nor will the desert heat or the sun beat down on them.
He who has compassion on them will guide them and lead them beside springs of **water.**

Five
Jeremiah 31:9
They will come with weeping; they will pray as I bring them back.
I will lead them beside streams of **water** on a level path where they will not stumble, because I am Israel's father, and Ephraim is my firstborn son.

Six
Mark 9:41
Truly I tell you, anyone who gives you a cup of **water** in my name because you belong to the Messiah will certainly not lose their reward.

Seven
Psalms 23:1-3a
The LORD is my shepherd; I lack nothing.
He makes me lie down in green pastures, he leads me beside quiet **waters**, he refreshes my soul.

Eight
Psalms 23:3b
He guides me along the right **paths** for his name's sake.

Nine
Matthew 6:11
Give us this day our daily **bread**.

Ten
Isaiah 43:2
When you pass through the **waters**, I will be with you; and when you pass through the rivers, they will not sweep over you.
When you **walk** through the fire, You will not be burned; the flames will not set you ablaze.

Eleven
Isaiah 58:11
The LORD will guide you always; he will satisfy your needs in a sun-scorched land and will strengthen your frame. You will be like a well-watered garden, like a spring whose **waters** never fail.

Twelve
Romans 14:14
As one who is in the Lord Jesus, I am fully convinced that no **food** is unclean in itself.

Thirteen
Mark 7:18-19
"Don't you see that nothing that enters a person from the outside can defile them? For it doesn't go into their heart but into their stomach, and then out of the body." (In saying this, Jesus declared all **foods** clean.)

Fourteen
Psalms 27:14
Wait for the LORD; be **strong** and take heart And wait for the LORD.

Fifteen
Isaiah 30:15
"In repentance and rest is your salvation, in quietness and trust is your **strength,** but you would have none of it."

Sixteen
Deuteronomy 33:25
The bolts of your gates will be iron and bronze, and your **strength** will equal your days.

Seventeen
Matthew 10:22
You will be hated by everyone because of me, but the one who **endures** to the end will be saved.

Eighteen
1 Samuel 2:30
Those who **honor** me I will honor, but those who despise me will be disdained.

Nineteen
Psalms 84:11
For the LORD God is a sun and shield; The LORD bestows favor and **honor**; no good thing does he withhold From those whose walk is blameless.

Twenty
Luke 14:8
"When someone invites you to a wedding feast, do not take the place of **honor**, for a person more distinguished than you may have been invited."

Twenty-one
Psalms 4:8
In **peace,** I will lie down and **sleep**, for you alone, LORD, make me dwell in safety.

Twenty-two
2 Chronicles 20:15
'Do not be afraid or discouraged because of this vast army. For the **battle** is not yours, but God's.'

Twenty-three
Psalms 37:7
Be **still** before the Lord and wait patiently for him; do not fret when people succeed in their ways, when they carry out their wicked schemes.

Twenty-four
2 Timothy 4:8
Now there is in store for me the crown of righteousness, which the Lord, the righteous Judge, will **award** to me on that day— and not only to me, but also to all who have longed for his appearing.

Twenty-five
Daniel 4:22
Your Majesty, you are that tree! You have become great and **strong**; your greatness has grown until it reaches the sky, and your dominion extends to distant parts of the earth.

Twenty-six
Isaiah 46:4
I have made you and I will **carry** you; I will sustain you, and I will rescue you.

Twenty-seven
1 Kings 22:15
But Jehoshaphat also said to the king of Israel, "First seek the **counsel** of the LORD."

Twenty-eight
Daniel 10:18-19a
Again the one who looked like a man touched me and gave me **strength**. "Do not be afraid, you who are highly esteemed," he said. "**Peace**! Be strong now; be strong."

Twenty-nine
Daniel 10:19b
When he spoke to me, I was strengthened and said, "Speak, my lord, since you have given me **strength**."

Thirty
Psalms 73:24
You guide me with your **counsel**, and afterward, you will take me into glory.

Thirty-one
Mark 6:50
Immediately he spoke to them and said, "Take **courage**! It is I. Don't be afraid."

Thirty-two
1 Corinthians 16:13
Be on your guard; stand firm in the faith; be **courageous**; be **strong**.

Thirty-three
Deuteronomy 31:23
The LORD gave this command to Joshua son of Nun: "Be **strong** and **courageous**, for you will bring the Israelites into the land I promised them on oath, and I myself will be with you."

Thirty-four
Joshua 10:25
Joshua said to them, "Do not be afraid; do not be discouraged. Be **strong** and **courageous**. This is what the LORD will do to all the enemies you are going to fight."

Thirty-five
Proverbs 22:3
The prudent see **danger** and take refuge, But the simple keep going and suffer for it.

Thirty-six
Proverbs 31:25
She is clothed with **strength** and dignity; She can laugh at the days to come.

Thirty-seven
Proverbs 13:4
A sluggard's appetite is never filled, But the desires of the **diligent** are fully satisfied.

Thirty-eight
Proverbs 1:1-6
The proverbs of Solomon son of David, king of Israel:
for gaining wisdom and **discipline;** for understanding words of insight; for receiving instruction in prudent behavior, doing what is right and just and fair; for giving prudence to those who are simple, knowledge and discretion to the young— let the wise listen and add to their learning, and let the discerning get guidance— for understanding proverbs and parables, the sayings and riddles of the wise.

Thirty-nine
Isaiah 28:16
So this is what the Sovereign LORD says:
"See, I lay a stone in Zion, a tested stone, a precious cornerstone for a sure foundation; The one who **trusts** will never be stricken with panic."

Forty
2 Thessalonians 3:13
And as for you, brothers and sisters, never **tire** of doing what is good.

Forty-one
Exodus 14:14
"The LORD will **fight** for you; you need only to be still."

Forty-two
1 Timothy 6:12
Fight the good fight of the faith. Take hold of the eternal life to which you were called when you made your good confession in the presence of many witnesses.

Forty-three
Joshua 7:19
Then Joshua said to Achan, "My son, give **glory** to the LORD, the God of Israel, and **honor** him. Tell me what you have done; do not hide it from me."

Forty-four
Proverbs 22:1
A good name is more desirable than great riches; To be esteemed is better than silver or **gold**.

Forty-five
Haggai 2:8
'The silver is mine, and the **gold** is mine,' declares the LORD Almighty.

Forty-six
Proverbs 16:24
Gracious words are a honeycomb, sweet to the soul and **healing** to the bones.

Forty-seven
Isaiah 58:8
Then your light will break forth like the dawn, and your **healing** will quickly appear; Then your righteousness will go before you, And the glory of the LORD will be your rear guard.

Forty-eight
Psalms 23:5
You prepare a **table** before me in the presence of my enemies. You anoint my head with oil; my cup overflows.

Forty-nine
Malachi 4:2
But for you who fear my name the sun of righteousness shall rise, with **healing** in its wings. You shall go forth **leaping** like calves from the stall.

Fifty
Proverbs 19:19
A **hot-tempered** person must pay the penalty; Rescue them, and you will have to do it again.

Fifty-one
Proverbs 19:20
Listen to **advice** and accept discipline, And at the end, you will be counted among the wise.

Fifty-two
Acts 10:14-15
"Surely not, Lord!" Peter replied. "I have never **eaten** anything impure or unclean." The voice spoke to him a second time, "Do not call anything impure that God has made clean."

Fifty-three
1 Thessalonians 5:6
And we urge you, brothers and sisters, to warn those who are idle and disruptive, **encourage** the disheartened, help the **weak**, and be **patient** with everyone.

Fifty-four
1 Corinthians 10:14
Therefore, my dear friends, flee from **idolatry.**

Fifty-five
Luke 1:37
"For nothing is **impossible** for God"

Fifty-six
Luke 18:27
Jesus replied, "What is **impossible** with man is **possible** with God."

Fifty-seven
Matthew 19:26
Jesus looked at them and said, "With man, this is **impossible**, but with God, all things are **possible**."

Fifty-eight
Mark 9:23
"If you can?" said Jesus. "Everything is **possible** for one who believes."

Fifty-nine
Psalms 23:6
Surely your **goodness** and love will follow me all the days of my life, and I will dwell in the house of the LORD forever.

Sixty
Psalms 112:6-8
Surely the **righteous** will never be shaken; they will be remembered forever.
They will have no **fear** of bad news; their hearts are steadfast, trusting in the LORD.
Their hearts are secure, they will have no fear; in the end they will look in **triumph** on their foes.

Sixty-one
Proverbs 17:22
A cheerful **heart** is good medicine, but a crushed spirit dries up the bones.

Sixty-two
Psalms 104:34
May my **meditation** be pleasing to him, as I rejoice in the LORD.

Sixty-three
Proverbs 9:9
Instruct the **wise,** and they will be wiser still; Teach the righteous, and they will add to their learning.

Sixty-four
Proverbs 10:9
Whoever walks in integrity walks securely, But whoever takes crooked **paths** will be found out.

Sixty-five
2 Samuel 6:14-15
Wearing a linen ephod, David was dancing before the LORD with all his **might** while he and all Israel were bringing up the ark of the LORD with shouts and the sound of trumpets.

Sixty-six
Jerimiah 20:11
But the LORD is with me like a **mighty** warrior; So my persecutors will **stumble** and not prevail.
They will fail and be thoroughly disgraced; Their dishonor will never be forgotten.

Sixty-seven
2 Timothy 2:3
Endure hardship with us like a good soldier of Christ Jesus.

Sixty-eight
Acts 17:28
'For in him we live and **move** and have our being.' As some of your own poets have said, 'We are his offspring.'

Sixty-nine
Psalms 16:11
You make known to me the **path** of life; you will fill me with joy in your presence, with eternal pleasures at your right hand.

Seventy
Proverbs 15:19
The way of the sluggard is blocked with thorns, But the **path** of the upright is a highway.

Seventy-one
Isaiah 26:7
The **path** of the righteous is level; You, the Upright One, make the way of the righteous smooth.

Seventy-two
Proverbs 4:11
I instruct you in the way of wisdom And lead you along straight **paths.**

Seventy-three
Proverbs 19:11
A person's **wisdom** yields patience; It is to one's glory to overlook an offense.

Seventy-four
Proverbs 14:29
Whoever is **patient** has great understanding, But one who is **quick-tempered** displays folly.

Seventy-five
Proverbs 16:32
Better a **patient** person than a warrior, one with **self-control** than one who takes a city.

Seventy-six
Psalms 37:37
Consider the blameless, observe the **upright**; A future awaits those who seek **peace.**

Seventy-seven
Proverbs 14:30
A heart at **peace** gives life to the **body**, But envy rots the bones.

Seventy-eight
Proverbs 27:2
Let someone else **praise** you, and not your own mouth; An outsider, and not your own lips.

Seventy-nine
Philippians 4:6-7
Do not be anxious about anything, but in every situation, by prayer and petition, with thanksgiving, present your requests to God. And the **peace** of God, which transcends all understanding, will guard your hearts and your minds in Christ Jesus.

Eighty
1 Chronicles 5:20
He answered their prayers because they **trusted** in him.

Eighty-one
Psalms 19:14
May these words of my mouth and this meditation of my **heart** be pleasing in your sight, LORD, my Rock and my Redeemer.

Eighty-two
Proverbs 27:4
Anger is cruel and fury **overwhelming**, but who can stand before jealousy?

Eighty-three
Jeremiah 12:5
"If you have **raced** with men on foot and they have worn you out, how can you compete with horses?
If you stumble in safe country, how will you manage in the thickets by the Jordan?"

Eighty-four
Psalms 18:29
With your **help,** I can advance against a troop; With my God, I can **scale** a wall.

Eighty-five
Ecclesiastes 3:1
There is a time for everything, And a **season** for every activity under the heaven.

Eighty-six
Matthew 12:20
A bruised reed he will not break, and a smoldering wick he will not snuff out till he has brought justice through to **victory**.

Eighty-seven
1 Samuel 17:47
"All those gathered here will know that it is not by sword or spear that the LORD saves; for the **battle** is the LORD's, and he will give all of you into our hands."

Eighty-eight
1 Samuel 10:26
Saul also went to his home in Gibeah, accompanied by **valiant** men whose **hearts** God had touched.

Eighty-nine
Isaiah 2:3
"He will teach us his ways so that we may **walk** in his **paths**."

Ninety
Isaiah 2:5
Come, descendants of Jacob, Let us **walk** in the light of the LORD.

Ninety-one
Daniel 4:37
Now I, Nebuchadnezzar, praise and exalt and glorify the King of heaven because everything he does is right and all his ways are just. And for those who **walk** in **pride**, he is able to **humble**.

Ninety-two
Ezra 10:4
"Rise up; this matter is in your hands. We will support you, so take **courage** and do it."

Ninety-three
Michah 6:8
He has shown you, O mortal, what is good.
And what does the LORD require of you?
To act justly and to love mercy And to **walk humbly** with
your God.

Ninety-four
Luke 7:19
Then he said to him, "Rise and go; your **faith** has made you
well."

Ninety-five
James 5:15
And the prayer offered in **faith** will make the sick person well;
the Lord will raise them up.

Ninety-six
Proverbs 19:2
Zeal without **knowledge** is not good— How much more will
hasty feet miss the way?

Ninety-seven
Romans 12:11
Never be lacking in **zeal,** but keep your spiritual fervor,
serving the Lord.

Ninety-eight
Galatians 4:18
It is fine to be **zealous**, provided the purpose is good, and to
be so always, not just when I am with you.

Ninety-nine
Romans 12:3
For by the grace given me, I say to every one of you: Do not think of yourself more highly than you ought but rather think of yourself with sober **judgment**, in accordance with the faith God has distributed to each of you. Just as each of us has one **body** with many members, and these members do not all have the same function, so in Christ we, though many, form one body, and each member belongs to all the others. We have different gifts according to the grace given to each of us.

One hundred
1 Corinthians 12:14
Even so the **body** is not made up of one part but of many. Now if the foot should say, "Because I am not a hand, I do not belong to the body," it would not for that reason stop being part of the body. And if the ear should say, "Because I am not an eye, I do not belong to the body," it would not for that reason stop being part of the body. If the whole body were an eye, where would the sense of hearing be? If the whole body were an ear, where would the sense of smell be? But in fact God has placed the parts in the body, every one of them, just as he wanted them to be. If they were all one part, where would the body be? As it is, there are many parts, but one body.

Subject Index

Confidence(ent)	3/29, 5/22, 8/1-6, 8/8, 8/11-16, 8/18-22
Counsel	BE27, BE30
Courage(ous)	2/12, 2/16-17, 2/23, 10/27, 10/30, BE31-34, BE92
Course	7/23
Created	11/21
Crown(s)(ed)	1/14-18
Danger	BE35
Diligent	BE37
Discipline	BE38
Eat(en)	BE52
Encourage(ment)	2/8, 2/27-28, 5/13, BE53
Endure(s)(ed)(ance)	1/3, 1/18, 2/6, 2/10, 2/27-28, 3/1-3/3, 3/5-7, 3/9-11, 3/13-15, 3/21, 4/26, 5/12, 5/13, BE17, BE67
Energy	11/10
Faith	BE94-95

Overwhelming	BE82
Path(s)	BE8, BE64, BE69-72, BE89
Patience	2/10, BE53, BE74-75
Peace	9/15, 12/26, BE21, BE28, BE76-77, BE79
Persevere(s)(ed)(ance)	3/15, 5/12, 7/4-5, 7/7-13, 7/15, 11/8, 11/15, 12/28
Physical	10/15
Plans	7/25-30
Possible	BE56-58
Power(ful)(fully)	2/10, 2/17, 5/16, 5/23-31, 6/1-3, 6/5-11, 9/2-3
Powerless	6/11
Praise	BE78
Pride(Proud)(ly)	5/15, 7/19, 10/3-6, 11/19-20, 11/22-26, BE91
Prosper(ous)(ed)(ity)	11/27-28, 11/30, 12/1-12/17
Quiet	1/22, 5/14

	6/17, 6/19, 9/4-5, 10/27, 10/29-30, BE14-16, BE25, BE28-29, BE32-34, BE36
Straining	7/6
Struggling	11/10
Stumble(ed)(ing)	7/21, 9/6-14, 9/16-22, BE66
Success(ful)(Succeed)	7/25, 10/24-31,11/1
Suffer(ing)	11/2-7, 11/11, 11/16
Swift	12/19
Table	BE48
Tired	5/9, BE40
Train(ed)(ing)	4/21, 8/10, 10/16, 10/18-19
Triumph	BE60
Trusts(ed)	3/24, BE39, BE80
Upright	BE76
Valiant	BE88
Victory(ies)('s)	6/18-24, 11/16, BE86

Walk	1/9, 5/3, BE10, BE89-91, BE 93
Water(s)	1/9, BE1-7, BE10-11
Weak(ness)(nesses)	1/5, 1/30, 5/16-22, 10/9, BE53
Weary(ies)	5/9-12
Wisdom(wise)	1/22, 2/19, 3/20, 3/23, 11/12, 12/27, 12/30-31, BE63, BE73
Zeal(ous)	BE96-98